Too Much to Carry Alone

OTHER TIME OUT CLASSICS

Keeping It Together in a Pull-Apart World
Mary Ellen Edmunds

Redefining Joy in the Last Days
Chris Stewart

Confessions of an Unbalanced Woman
Emily Watts

Believe in What You're Doing, Believe in Who You Are
Hilary Weeks

When Your Prayers Seem Unanswered
S. Michael Wilcox

Too Much to Carry Alone

CAMILLE FRONK OLSON

DESERET
BOOK

SALT LAKE CITY, UTAH

Library of Congress Cataloging-in-Publication Data
Olson, Camille Fronk.
   Too much to carry alone / Camille Fronk Olson.
      p. cm.
   Includes bibliographical references.
   ISBN 978-1-60641-036-3 (hardbound : alk. paper)
   1. Christian life—Mormon authors.   2. Jesus Christ—Mormon interpretations.   I. Title.
   BX8656.O53   2009
   248.4'89332—dc22
                                                                    2008042846

Printed in the United States of America
R. R. Donnelley, Crawfordsville, IN

10   9   8   7   6   5   4   3   2   1

Discipleship

After hearing the Savior's Bread of Life sermon, many in His Galilean audience recoiled at the "hard saying" He required if they would truly become His disciples (John 6:60). When Jesus then asked His apostles whether they too would walk "no more with him," Simon Peter responded, "Lord, to whom shall we go? thou hast the words of eternal life" (John 6:66, 68).

The prophet Nephi expressed a similar witness. Feeling the weight of new leadership responsibilities at the death of his father, Lehi, Nephi sensed his inadequacy because his weaknesses and sins had become all too apparent to him. In distress he cried out, "O wretched man that I am! . . . I am encompassed about, because of the temptations and the sins which do so easily beset me." Yet Nephi also recognized that discipleship with Jesus Christ was the only way he could successfully guide his people. In almost the same breath, he exclaimed, "Nevertheless, I know in whom I have trusted. My God hath been my support; he hath led me through mine afflictions. . . . He hath filled me with his love" (2 Nephi 4:17–21).

The apostle Paul, surrounded by opposition against the doctrines of the gospel, articulated his discipleship with the Lord in this powerful statement: "I can do all things through Christ which strengtheneth me" (Philippians 4:13).

These scriptural examples and many more illustrate the confidence, empowerment, and direction that come when we wholeheartedly turn our lives over to the Lord and become His disciples. A disciple of Jesus Christ is one who has gained a witness through the Spirit of the divinity and mission of the Savior, studies His gospel, incorporates His teachings into daily life by relying on His enabling power, and spreads the news of His gospel to others. Disciples of Christ are not without weaknesses or sin, but their shortcomings neither paralyze them nor prevent them from selfless service and daily repentance. The goal of a disciple is not to be different from everyone else but to be more like the Master. Likewise, discipleship is not in praying that God be for us but rather in praying that we be for Him. Not a single event, discipleship with Christ is a process that continues throughout life and deepens humility and gratitude all along the way.

Peace in
Uncertain Times

Scriptural examples demonstrate that discipleship is not a promise of protection from pain, hardships, and disappointment. True disciples know that a sinless life was realized only once in mortality. Their faith in the perfect One fills them with joy and strength to carry on and find hope even in uncertain times. The apostle Paul observed, "For I have learned, in whatsoever state I am, therewith to be content. . . . every where and in all things I am instructed both to be full and to be hungry, both to abound and to suffer need" (Philippians 4:11–12). Through years of discipleship, Paul had learned that joy and fulfillment come through a testimony of the Redeemer, not from an elevated standing in the world.

When he wrote his letter to the Philippians, Paul had not just received wonderful news or accomplished a great feat. He had not recently learned that he had been awarded the Nobel Peace Prize or converted the entire Jewish Sanhedrin to faith in Christ. No, Paul wrote this epistle when he was a prisoner in Rome. His claim that he had learned to be content in all circumstances carries authenticity because at the time he wrote it, his life was not ideal by any definition. And yet Paul had found opportunities to spread the gospel among the empire's leaders, precisely because he was a prisoner in Caesar's headquarters (Philippians 1:12–19). In other words, because Paul was imprisoned in Rome, he could fulfill the Lord's command to preach His gospel to "kings" (Acts 9:15). With the strength of the Lord, Paul accomplished all that He asked.

A modern-day example of discipleship is Sahar Qumsiyeh, a Palestinian member of The Church of Jesus Christ of Latter-day Saints. Like the apostle Paul, Sahar has learned to find divine strength in extremely challenging circumstances. I first met Sahar in 1999 when I was a member of the Jerusalem Branch and was assigned to visit teach her at her home in Beit Sahour, just outside Bethlehem. Sahar had become acquainted with the Church after she accepted a scholarship to Brigham Young University. She was baptized in Provo in 1996, shortly before she graduated with a master's degree in statistics. I have kept all of Sahar's e-mail communications because they remind me of the strength and courage that come through discipleship with the Redeemer.

Upon returning to Palestine after her baptism, Sahar faced disappointment and confusion from her family as well as uncertainty and danger in traveling the short distance to attend church services at the BYU Jerusalem Center each week. The Center is only seven miles from Sahar's home, but because Israeli laws restrict and often forbid Palestinians who are not residents of Jerusalem from entering the city, Sahar has been forced to find alternative routes to church. She writes, "I have had to sneak out and avoid being seen by the Israeli soldiers. This process involved going up a nearby hill and around the checkpoint. I sometimes had to hide behind trees and rocks waiting for the soldiers to move so I could pass, but somehow I have always made it to church."

Her circuitous trek usually requires at least three hours. In the rainy season, Sahar has hiked through muddy fields. During the construction of the wall that the Israelis built around Jerusalem, a hole less than a foot in diameter was the only way to reach the other side. Sahar shimmied through in order not to miss receiving the sacrament and renewing her covenants with the Lord. Other times, she has passed by soldiers without being stopped while those around her were turned back. She writes, "It was as though I were invisible."

Sahar speaks of these numerous challenging experiences. "Some might say that living like this must be hard. It is not! When I look back at all these times, I think that they are among the happiest days of my life. The reason is that I have the Holy Ghost with me as my constant companion."

Each Christmas and Easter, Sahar sends a special

holiday greeting to a large number of friends. She often mentions the absence of peace, hope, and love between the religious groups in that land. "As we celebrate the birth of our Lord and Savior Jesus Christ, the Prince of Peace," Sahar wrote one Christmas, "some wonder if peace is possible in this country. But I have felt His peace right here in the midst of all the conflict. There may not be peace in this land, but there is peace in me, only because of the Prince of Peace."

Both Sahar and the apostle Paul bear witness that salvation comes through the grace of Jesus Christ, not by our works. They also know that what we do with our God-given time and talents is very important to the Lord. When our faith in the Savior is unshakable, we cannot be stopped from efforts to help others discover the blessings of the Atonement and the abundant life. As we become true disciples of Jesus Christ, we experience a deeper reverence and gratitude for His commandments and purer motives to obey them. Even after all we can do to obey the Lord, He is the enabling source for all our good works and the power behind all our successes.

When we are honest, we acknowledge that mortality requires too much for us to carry alone. As His disciples, however, He makes all things possible when we take His yoke upon us.

Scriptural Focus

God's desire for us is not merely to return to Him but to return as new creatures, changed from our fallen natures to become spiritually born of God. He sent His son and numerous prophets to teach us to become true disciples of Christ.

The Savior invites all men and women everywhere to be born again and become His disciples. During His mortal ministry, He taught us how that process of becoming occurs and what costs are required of us. Matthew 11:28–30 is an excellent example. These three verses contain the Savior's invitation, our responsibility in the process (the cost), and

His enduring promise that we will not be left to carry our burdens alone:

> Come unto me *[the invitation]*,
> all ye that labour and are heavy laden
> *[our condition without the Savior]*,
> and I will give you rest *[the promise]*.

> Take my yoke upon you, and learn of me;
> for I am meek and lowly in heart
> *[the cost]*:
> and ye shall find rest unto your souls
> *[the promise repeated]*.

> For my yoke is easy, and my burden is light
> *[a contrast to burdens we are currently
> carrying]*.

Let us explore each of these concepts.

"Come unto Me"

The scriptures are replete with teachings that Christ is "no respecter of persons" (Acts 10:34; see also Acts 10:35; Romans 2:11; 1 Nephi 17:35). We are touched by His compassion to Jew and Gentile, to the sick, and to the outcast. He healed women and men, Samaritan and Pharisee, publican and harlot. His invitation for the great blessing of "rest" was likewise not restricted to a representative sample of people or to those with the right pedigree or to those living in a particular area during a particular time. His invitation was—and is—to all.

At times the Savior expanded the invitation to

come and see, underscoring the opportunity for each individual to experience His message firsthand. We can never know Him, trust Him, and willingly follow Him if we do not first come to Him and see what He alone can offer us.

John the Baptist understood this critical step in discipleship. He sent his followers to experience for themselves the power and majesty of Jesus. Only then could they see and hear that there was one greater than John. When John the Baptist was in prison, he assigned his disciples to go to Jesus and ask, "Art thou he that should come? or look we for another?" (Luke 7:19; see also Matthew 11:2–3).

John knew the identity of the Savior but wanted his followers to likewise learn the truth from the Spirit. After their association with Jesus Christ, they could then return to John and report the tremendous things they had seen and heard.

The words *Visitors Welcome* are posted on the exterior of all meetinghouses of The Church of Jesus Christ of Latter-day Saints, reminding visitors and members alike that Christ's invitation, "Come unto me," is still applicable today. Furthermore, before we make covenants with the Lord, we have occasion to "see" the Savior and witness that He is the Redeemer of the world. Before we are baptized or enter one of the Lord's temples, we testify that we know and have felt, through a personal witness from the Spirit of God, that the teachings of Jesus are true. We cannot talk about, let alone appreciate, the costs of true discipleship unless we have first come to Christ and received a testimony of His divinity and goodness. He never commits us to discipleship until we have an established trust in Him.

Specifically, the Savior invites those "that labour and are heavy laden" to come unto Him (Matthew 11:28). Who among us is exempt from this description? As fallen creatures, we all carry burdens or challenges that often defy resolution. By accepting the Lord's invitation to come to Him, we encounter the way to resolve every one of our problems. We are not talking about temporary, Band-Aid treatments here but eternal solutions. Each of us is personally invited to come unto Christ and trust Him to heal us. That is where the cost, or "yoke," comes in.

The Yoke

The most commonly recognized yoke is a wooden beam that is worn on the shoulders of a pair of oxen or other draft animals. Working together as a team, two oxen pull extremely heavy loads with their massive, broad shoulders. Many early Latter-day Saint pioneers depended on teams of yoked oxen to carry their belongings across the plains to the Salt Lake Valley.

A man from my hometown, who owns an extensive collection of wagons and horse-drawn carriages, suggested to me another use of yokes. After showing me all his wagons, including some yokes made for animals, I asked him his thoughts about the scripture in Matthew 11. He pointed out numerous archaic tools that adorned a wall of his home. Among them was a yoke designed to be worn by a person. He suggested that the yoke in the Savior's teaching was a yoke to be worn by humans rather than work animals.

This human yoke is a crossbar fitted to a person's shoulders with ropes or cables hanging from the ends, to which buckets or baskets are attached for carrying loads. A yoke allows a person to carry heavy burdens for a longer period of time. In other words, such a tool gives individuals endurance to perform life's labors. The yoke distributes the weight of a balanced load over the broadest and strongest part of the body—the shoulders—enabling individuals to use their entire body, braced by the spinal column, to support the shoulders in labor.

The advantage of carrying heavy loads with a yoke is best seen when compared to other ways of transporting weighty and cumbersome burdens. When we hold a loaded basket in our extended hand, or sling it over the end of one shoulder, or dangle it

Photo by Chad Emmett; used by permission.

around our neck, we quickly realize how uncomfortable and taxing it is to our hand, arm, shoulder, or neck. In each of these cases, all the weight is concentrated at one point, causing extensive stress to that one part of the body. Yokes diffuse that stress and make it more bearable.

Historically, yokes for humans were used for evil purposes. Conquering armies put yokes on their captives to subject them to humiliation and forced labor.

A tongue connected to a wagon or other load could be attached to the yoke, requiring the captive to take the role of a work animal in heavy labor. Perhaps the children of Israel, as slaves in Egypt, wore such yokes to build the massive monuments and buildings of Pharaoh's glorious cities before Moses delivered them.

From ancient murals carved in stone depicting the Assyrians' victories in the eighth century before Christ, we know that the Assyrians used yokes to harness and drive their captives. At the same time the prophet Isaiah was teaching the Israelites in Judah, the Assyrian army was capturing the people of the northern kingdom of Israel and removing them from their homelands so that the Assyrians could occupy the land themselves. Although the Israelites of the northern kingdom had turned from the Lord and followed after other gods, Isaiah promised that the Lord had not forgotten these scattered ten tribes. Isaiah powerfully testified, "The Lord of hosts hath sworn, saying, . . . I will break the Assyrian in my land, and upon my mountains tread him under foot: then shall his yoke

Assyrian bas-relief of yoked captives.
Sketch by Ashton Young; used by permission.

depart from off them, and his burden depart from off their shoulders" (Isaiah 14:24–25).

We can see that a yoke may symbolize either slavery and oppression or empowerment beyond a person's natural abilities. In reality, every one of us wears a figurative yoke as we attempt to carry the responsibilities and burdens of life. Often the load we carry is oppressive. We are therefore among those whom Jesus described as "all ye that labour and are heavy laden." In Matthew 11:28–30, however, the Lord teaches us how to carry our burdens successfully so that they actually become light.

"All Ye That Labour and Are Heavy Laden"

Let us take a look at these burdens we are carrying. What is causing us to be heavy laden today? I do not pretend to be able to name all burdens in a finite list, but several examples may help us to recognize clearly that in this scripture the Savior is talking to each one of us. Arguably, the heaviest burden is sin. When we know "to do good" but "[do] it not" (James 4:17), or when we knowingly commit evil, we offend the Spirit of God and are left to our own strength.

We can be cumbered with heavy burdens of other kinds as well. Financial concerns are particularly weighty, whether we have spent more than we can repay, or we have never had what we need to properly care for our own, or we have too much and do not know how best to use it. Other burdens may involve fear of the future, worries about being alone, attempts to live up to others' expectations, or browbeating ourselves for falling short of our own impossible expectations. We become heavy laden when we continually compare ourselves to a neighbor who appears to have it all together while we are filled with ignorance and doubt, or when we get sucked into the relentless pursuit of status or wealth, or when, as a new convert in the Church, we feel inferior and lost because we don't speak or understand the Latter-day Saint cultural lingo.

The heavy laden include those who have not accepted or acknowledged the enabling power of Jesus Christ; who suffer from illness, betrayal, persecution, loneliness, irony, or unreciprocated love; or who have concern for a loved one living in a nation at war; and so forth. Our burdens are heavy when we are bent under the pressures of time and have lost perspective concerning priorities and rest. At times, service in the

Church, care of our families, and even worship of God can feel heavy and cumbersome.

When the Savior taught the sermon recorded in Matthew 11, He was addressing a group of Jews who were weighed down with the minute particulars of what had become the redefined law of Moses. The law's demands, reshaped and embellished by scribes and Pharisees, had become impossible to obey successfully. Even Peter, as head of the Church after the Lord's resurrection, referred to the law of Moses as "a yoke upon the neck of the disciples, which neither our fathers nor we were able to bear" (Acts 15:10). Jesus chastened the scribes and Pharisees of His day who continued to subject the Jews to their interpretation of the law and yet refused to give any support to assist them. He warned, "For they bind heavy burdens and grievous to be borne, and lay them on men's shoulders; but they themselves will not move them with one of their fingers" (Matthew 23:4).

To the humble Jews who heard Jesus teach in mortality and to us who are likewise heavy laden, the Lord calls, "Come, . . . every one that thirsteth, come ye to the waters; and he that hath no money, come buy and eat; yea, come buy wine and milk without money and without price" (2 Nephi 9:50; see also Isaiah 55:1).

These great promises are totally without price as far as money or material possessions are concerned, but they are not without cost in terms of our priorities and desires. When we finally acknowledge that we have too much to carry alone, we hear the Lord's invitation to willingly take, not just any yoke, but specifically *His* yoke upon us. To accept His yoke means that we will have to set aside the faulty, yet by now very familiar, yoke we have been using and trust in His liberating gospel.

"Take My Yoke upon You"

Willingly taking His yoke upon us at first appears ludicrous when we have too much to carry already. Perhaps, we may reason, Christ promises us that our burdens will become light with His yoke, because, like an Aesop's fable, when He finally removes the yoke, our former problems will feel light in comparison. Or maybe we hope it means that we simply deposit all our responsibilities and cares upon the Lord and leap off to play, never turning back to see if all is well. But neither of these assumptions is what the Lord is offering. He sees greater potential in us than we ever perceive in ourselves. He also knows what is necessary to help us reach that potential.

What, then, makes His yoke different from the others? He told us that His "yoke is easy" and His "burden is light." In this passage from Matthew 11:30, the Greek word translated *easy* means "kindly." One way that yokes can be made more kindly is to fit them properly. Ill-fitting yokes may be rough-hewn, causing chafed necks and gouged shoulders. A yoke may also be too long and therefore concentrate too much weight on the ends of the shoulders. As a carpenter by trade, Jesus likely made yokes for both animals and people who had heavy burdens to carry. He knew that the most kindly yokes would be sanded smooth to protect the parts of the body they touched rather than cause sore spots. He knew that a strong yet flexible wood could receive a design in which the yoke bowed slightly in the center, relieving pressure from the neck when heavy burdens were attached. Jesus also knew about the importance of having the load perfectly balanced when it is attached to the yoke. The Savior knows a lot about perfect balance.

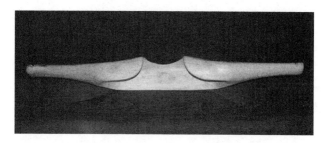

Yoke carved by Blaine Wilcox.
Photo by Chris Gardner; used by permission.

Elder Spencer H. Osborn, formerly a member of the Seventy, shared an observation about yokes while traveling in the Philippines. He passed a farmer "carrying an enormous load of vegetables and produce hanging from both ends of a wooden yoke carried across his shoulders." After Elder Osborn stopped to take the farmer's picture, the man lowered his burden to visit. Elder Osborn reported their conversation: "I asked my friend if his load wasn't really too heavy to carry a great distance. He replied, 'No, it isn't, because it's balanced.'

"'Doesn't that yoke hurt?' I asked.

"'At first it did, but I carved and sanded it with a

rough stone, and now it fits and is comfortable'" (*Ensign,* November 1984, 76).

When my friend with the wagon collection showed me the yoke made for a person to wear, he invited me to put it on my shoulders. The yoke had been hollowed out to fit around the shoulders and was carved and sanded smoothly to go behind the neck without rubbing. I was surprised at how comfortable it was. When he pulled down on the ropes attached to the ends of the yoke, I could feel the added weight, but it didn't hurt.

I asked my brother, who is a mechanical engineer, about the dynamics of a yoke that allows someone to carry such remarkable loads. He helped me to understand the optimum design of a yoke, including the importance of a balanced load. When the load attached to the yoke is uneven, the person is thrown off balance and must use his or her energy to compensate. More specifically, torque is forced upon the spinal column, causing instant and sustained discomfort that requires the person to use extra exertion to counterbalance the load and restore a semblance of equilibrium.

A knowledgeable carpenter could design and create the perfect yoke for an individual, one that precisely fits the person's frame, and could calculate a balanced load considering the person's height, weight, and strength. Jesus Christ, the Master Carpenter, fulfills those expectations and more. He designs a yoke for each of us that not only fits our physical stature but considers our personality, talents, and personal circumstances. President Howard W. Hunter taught of the Lord's sensitivity to the personalized loads we carry:

"Obviously, the personal burdens of life vary from person to person, but every one of us has them. Furthermore, each trial in life is tailored to the individual's capacities and needs as known by a loving Father in Heaven. Of course, some sorrows are brought on by the sins of a world not following the counsel of that Father in Heaven. Whatever the reason, none of us seems to be completely free from life's challenges. To one and all, Christ said, in effect: As long as we all must bear some burden and shoulder some yoke, why not let it be mine? My promise to you is that my yoke is easy, and my burden is light. (See Matt. 11:28–30.)" (*Ensign*, November 1990, 18).

To understand more about the nature of burdens, let's consider two false assumptions that, if pursued, may block our access to the Lord's divine assistance and keep us from accepting His yoke.

We can avoid tribulation

The first false assumption is that if we are good enough, we can avoid bad things happening to us and those we love. If we can just keep all the commandments and pay an honest tithing and have daily prayer and scripture study, we can appease God, earn His good pleasure, and thereby assure ourselves of His protection from heartache, accident, or tragedy. When such thinking drives us, Elder Neal A. Maxwell observed, we "want victory without battle and expect campaign ribbons merely for watching" (*Men and Women of Christ* [Salt Lake City: Bookcraft, 1991], 2).

Trials will surely come, including when we are trying to do everything right. Elder Richard G. Scott observed that one purpose of adversity is "to accomplish the Lord's own purposes in our life that we may receive the refinement that comes from testing." Then he warned, "Just when all seems to be going right, challenges often come in multiple doses applied simultaneously" (*Ensign,* November 1995, 16).

If we hold the belief that God will shield us from tribulation because of our obedience and then adversity strikes, we may be tempted to accuse God of not hearing our prayers, or worse, of not honoring His promises. Obedience to God is not insurance against pain and sadness. Some unpleasant things just come with this telestial turf. Challenges have always been included in God's great plan to test our faith, to stimulate in us growth, humility, and compassion. Heartache and struggle were divinely designed to stretch us to the point where we have nowhere to turn but to God. Christ heals our pain; He does not prevent it.

Scriptures remind us that the faithful are frequently stretched to greater devotion and humility by divinely designed trials. For example, the ground was cursed for Adam's sake, and Eve was promised that her sorrow (or hardships) would be multiplied (Genesis 3:16–17). The apostle Paul acknowledged, "There was given to me a thorn in the flesh, . . . to buffet me, lest I should be exalted above measure" (2 Corinthians 12:7). After she left the comforts of her Jerusalem home to sojourn in the wilderness, the Lord presented Sariah with a greater test when He commanded her to send all four of her sons back to Jerusalem to face those who desired her husband's death (1 Nephi 5:1–8).

Christ's mission was never to prevent hearts from breaking but to heal broken hearts. He came to wipe away our tears, not to ensure that we would never weep. He clearly promised, "In the world ye shall have tribulation" (John 16:33).

Trusting in our own efforts

The second false assumption we may have when we accept the Lord's yoke can be just as destructive to our faith in Him as the first false assumption. We may conclude that hardships come because we haven't done *enough* good in the world.

When considering tribulation and the Lord's

Atonement from this perspective, we can look at the scripture "It is by grace that we are saved, after all we can do" (2 Nephi 25:23) and deduce that we must first prove our worth through our obedience and our righteousness before the Lord's sacrifice will cover us or His grace enable us. Trusting in our own efforts rather than humbly acknowledging God is reflected in the term "*self*-righteousness."

When we look through the lens of our righteousness and take comfort in our good efforts, the idea of depending wholly on Christ and accepting His yoke (2 Nephi 31:19; Moroni 6:4) seems a bit risky. Consider the domino-like sentiments such a perspective can produce: What if I depend on God but He doesn't answer me when I need His immediate help? With all the serious problems in the universe, why would He have time or interest in my personal crisis? Then again, if I organize my life carefully and think smart, I could resist temptation and not have to lean upon the Lord for help at all. I will then not be one of those who contributed to His suffering in Gethsemane. If I just use my skills and genius I can actually help the Lord rather than draw on His strength. After all, so many people around here are in worse circumstances than I.

Unwittingly, when we reason this way, we sound eerily similar to Korihor's humanistic preaching in the Book of Mormon: "But every man fared in this life according to the management of the creature; therefore every man prospered according to his genius, and that every man conquered according to his strength," thereby showing that they had no need for Christ and His Atonement. "And thus [Korihor] did preach unto them, leading away the hearts of many, . . . yea, leading away many women, and also men, to commit whoredoms" (Alma 30:17–18).

When we become fearful and unsettled by the unexpected, our faith in Christ fades into gratifying our pride by our vain ambitions (D&C 121:37). Such thinking easily leads to justifying wrongdoing because we are in control—we know better than others, so sin is not a problem for us. Our efforts focus on personal success to show that we don't need anyone else. If we can just get control over our world—our addictions in all their varieties, our eating disorders and obsession with thinness, our insistence that our house always be immaculate, our fascination with outward evidence of education and success—then do we think we can finally feel good about ourselves? The scriptural listing of women before men in the reaction to Korihor's teachings is curious wording indeed. I don't know all that such wording could imply, but we can at least conclude that women were not exempt from Korihor's "management of the creature" philosophy and maybe were even particularly attracted to it.

Christ declared, "In the world ye shall have tribulation: but be of good cheer; *I* have overcome the world" (John 16:33; emphasis added). He didn't say *you* must overcome the world or that He overcame the world just for the weak ones who weren't smart enough or strong enough to do it on their own. He said, "*I* have overcome the world."

The Lord's yoke perfectly equalizes our individual responsibilities and personal burdens and distributes the weight so that it is not only bearable but easy. His yoke is not harsh, sharp, or debilitating but accommodating, encouraging, and enabling.

While doing research about yokes, I secretly hoped to find evidence that in some way a good yoke actually transferred the weight of the load someplace away from the person carrying it, freeing him or her from bearing the burden. If you are also hoping for such a discovery, I am sorry to report that I found no such magical solution. What I did find, however, is even better.

The Father did not send us to earth to learn how to escape burdens and responsibility. He sent us to decipher which of our burdens are unnecessary and debilitating, to learn how to divest ourselves of that extra baggage, and how to successfully carry our God-given loads. We are here to learn to become more like the Savior, and we don't do that by having someone else carry our burdens for us. The Lord's yoke not only enables us to carry the load He called us to assume but allows us to carry it for as long as He requires. As one biblical scholar described it, "The weight of Christ's yoke is wings to the soul" (George Arthur Buttrick et al., *Interpreter's Bible,* 12 vols. [New York: Abingdon Press, 1951–57], 7:391).

"My Yoke Is Easy, and My Burden Is Light"

Consider five ways in which the Lord lightens our burdens when we take His yoke upon us.

Disposing of unnecessary baggage

When we assume the Lord's yoke, we discover we are carrying a lot of unnecessary things. Often these are burdens we insisted on packing with us, even though they never helped us and they took up space needed for important cargo. Sins against God are the heavies that come first to mind. Once we repent of those favorite sins we think aren't adding much weight, we are amazed at how light the overall load suddenly becomes.

Next among baggage that must be discarded are sins we have repented of and for which we have already received the Lord's forgiveness. If we continue to cling to them, as though wearing a massive medallion of guilt, our load becomes overwhelmingly burdensome and heavy. Through His Atonement, Christ has already picked up these burdens and authorized us to let them go.

In addition, we need to jettison attitudes that insist we do things our way rather than the Lord's way and habits that encourage others to put energy-zapping burdens into our buckets. Besides adding excess weight, accepting others' defeating judgments makes our load immediately topsy-turvy, much like a washing machine shaking radically out of balance. President Spencer W. Kimball taught, "When you do not worry or concern yourself too much with what other people do and believe and say, there will come to you a new freedom" (*The Teachings of Spencer W.*

Kimball, ed. Edward L. Kimball [Salt Lake City: Bookcraft, 1982], 236).

Jesus Christ clearly taught that a person cannot "serve two masters: for either he will hate the one, and love the other; or else he will hold to the one, and despise the other" (Matthew 6:24; see also 3 Nephi 13:24). He also said, "They who are not for me are against me" (2 Nephi 10:16). President Brigham Young identified the chaos caused by insisting on carrying unnecessary burdens, whether burdens of our choosing or burdens chosen by someone other than the Lord: "They who try to serve God and still cling to the spirit of the world, have got on two yokes—the yoke of Jesus and the yoke of the devil, and they will have plenty to do. They will have a warfare inside and outside, and the labor will be very galling, for they are directly in opposition one to the other. Cast off the yoke of the enemy, and put on the yoke of Christ, and you will say that his yoke is easy and his burden is light. This I know by experience" (*Journal of Discourses,* 26 vols. [London: Latter-day Saints' Book Depot, 1854–86], 16:123).

Christ's yoke becomes easy and His burden light when we dispose of unnecessary baggage, including the yoke of Satan. The apostle Paul encouraged us to "lay aside every weight, and the sin which doth so easily beset us, and let us run with patience the race that is set before us" (Hebrews 12:1). From his perspective, eliminating Satan's yoke of bondage makes the burden so light we can even run while carrying the load.

Sustaining power through covenants

Covenants are "the primary force in [our] lives," taught Elder M. Russell Ballard (*Ensign,* May 1999, 86). When we make covenants with the Lord, He promises us His strength to support us in carrying our loads, thus making our burdens lighter. At baptism, we covenanted to be willing to take Christ's name upon us, or figuratively speaking, to take His yoke upon us. In return, the Lord promises that His Spirit will always be with us. In reality, we could not possibly handle the total weight of mortality without the Lord's support. The psalmist therefore counseled us to "cast thy burden upon the Lord, and he shall sustain thee" (Psalm 55:22). The fact that He sustains us suggests that we still carry His yoke, but we are not alone.

Neither are we merely appreciative spectators while He does all the work. The demands are real, so He promised He would not leave us comfortless (John 14:18). President Howard W. Hunter reasoned: "Why face life's burdens alone, Christ asks, or why face them with temporal support that will quickly falter? To the heavy laden it is Christ's yoke, it is the power and peace of standing side by side with a God that will provide the support, balance, and the strength to meet our challenges and endure our tasks here in the hardpan field of mortality" (*Ensign*, November 1990, 18).

That tremendous support is shown in a promise the Lord gave to missionaries in the early days of the Church: "And whoso receiveth you, there I will be also, for I will go before your face. I will be on your right hand and on your left, and my Spirit shall be in your hearts, and mine angels round about you, to bear you up" (D&C 84:88). That is some evidence of sustaining us in our burdens!

Mutual support

The covenant of baptism also includes a promise that we will watch out for each other and help where there is a need. The Lord's yoke is easy and His burden light because we have the Lord's sustaining power and help from each other in carrying our load. When we work together, we create a synergism in which each participant is strengthened and more is accomplished with significantly less stress or pressure on everyone's shoulders than when we work alone. In addition, when we vicariously feel the heartache of another, we often gain strength and wisdom from a particular trial without having to experience that trial ourselves.

As early as the Creation, we can see that the Lord never intended us to face the burdens of mortality alone. Eve was essential to the plan. She was identified by the Lord as a "help meet" for Adam (Moses 3:18; Genesis 2:18). An understanding of the original Hebrew words gives powerful insight to the meaning of the term and the reciprocal nature of men's and women's God-given abilities. The first word, translated as *help,* combines the meanings "to rescue or save" with the idea of "strength." The second word, translated as *meet,* means "equal." These words, considered together, suggest someone who has equal strength to rescue. In other words, the Lord provided Adam the partnership of Eve, who was given capacity to help Adam as he was given strength to help her. It is important to note that nowhere in scripture does the term *helpmate* appear. That term would suggest the Lord gave Adam a companion who would carry his load for him—quite a different meaning from that communicated by *help meet.*

Not everyone has a loyal spouse who provides the service of help meet. Nevertheless, the Lord has organized His Church so that we help each other carry burdens in additional ways. Consider the people of Alma, who desired to come unto Christ and take His yoke upon them. Consequently they covenanted "to bear one another's burdens, that they may be light; . . . and [were] willing to mourn with those that mourn; yea, and comfort those that stand in need of comfort" (Mosiah 18:8–9). When we make this same covenant with the Lord at baptism, we become members of a community of Saints who have all made the same covenant. When we faithfully keep that covenant, every individual in our ward or branch will feel the lift or boost that comes from the larger community. When we forget that covenant, individual brothers and sisters may feel overwhelmed and discouraged to the point that they will leave the yoke of Christ behind and search in vain for a seemingly easier way to carry their load.

Greater strength

Increased service in wearing the Lord's yoke gradually strengthens our back and shoulders so that we become capable of carrying greater loads and carrying them with greater ease. We all know that muscles that are consistently used and stretched become stronger, whereas those not used quickly atrophy. Likewise, if we go to the gym and ask for advice to increase our body's strength, the trainer may start us off with five-pound weights. After we master the five-pounders, the trainer is unlikely to say, "Okay, you're strong." She will probably hand us an additional five-pound weight and encourage us to lift ten or fifteen pounds.

Learning to wear the Lord's yoke is like being a new mother feeling completely overwhelmed at all her new responsibilities and wondering how she will ever have the energy or wisdom to nurture this baby to adulthood. Then she notices a mother with five children, and she is astonished. How does she do it? The mother of five will explain, "I got them one at a time." As we mature in the Lord's service, He increases the weight of our responsibility, and our overall strength increases as a result. We are learning to become more like Him.

Let's return to Alma and his covenant-keeping community of Saints, warned to leave the waters of Mormon and settle in Helam, outside the purview of their neighbors. They did not enjoy their Zionlike society undisturbed for long because they were discovered by a band of Lamanites and Alma's former associates, the wicked priests of Noah. Amulon, the chief of the wicked priests, immediately put these good people into bondage and "exercised authority over them, and put tasks upon them, and put taskmasters over them" (Mosiah 24:9).

But Alma and his people had already enjoyed many experiences carrying the yoke of Christ, so they were able to handle their captivity with remarkable grace. They knew the source of their strength, and they prayed continually, even when Amulon placed guards to try to stop them from praying. Because they had already recognized the Savior's grace in their lives, the Lord knew this experience could only strengthen them more. Naturally, the Lord remembered His covenant with them:

"And it came to pass [suggesting that some time has passed without any sign of divine assistance] that the voice of the Lord came to them in their afflictions, saying: Lift up your heads and be of good comfort, for I know of the covenant which ye have made unto me; and I will covenant with my people and deliver them out of bondage" (Mosiah 24:13).

Their complete release from bondage, however, was not imminent. First, the Lord told them that He would "ease the burdens which are put upon your shoulders, that even you cannot feel them upon your backs" (v. 14). Interestingly, the Lord did not ease their burdens by removing the yoke and the accompanying weight thrust upon them by their enemies. Again, the Lord had greater things in store for them than finding ways to escape responsibility and hardship. He was teaching them about godhood. Then we read: "It came to pass [more time passes] that the burdens which were laid upon Alma and his brethren were made light; yea, the Lord did strengthen them that they could bear up their burdens with ease, and they did submit cheerfully and with patience to all the will of the Lord" (v. 15). Alma's people were strengthened so that their burdens felt light.

What a stunning example of how the Lord incrementally strengthens us with His yoke to lighten our burdens. The Bible Dictionary teaches us that through the grace of Jesus Christ, not only does He provide His divine support and strength but we actually "receive strength and assistance to do good works that [we] otherwise would not be able to maintain if left to [our] own means" (LDS Bible Dictionary, s.v. "grace").

The burden is light because we have become stronger through the grace of God.

Carrying burdens the Lord's way

The Savior gave His own explanation in Matthew 11:29 for why His yoke is easy. He taught, "Take my yoke upon you, and learn of me; for I am meek and lowly in heart." It is instructive to note that in the Greek the Lord did not say, "Learn *of* me," but rather "learn *from* me." One biblical scholar observed: "The yoke . . . symbolized discipleship. When our Lord added the phrase 'learn from me,' the imagery would have been familiar to Jewish listeners. In ancient writings, a pupil who submitted himself to a teacher was said to take the teacher's yoke" (John A. McArthur Jr., *The Gospel According to Jesus* [Grand Rapids, Mich.: Zondervan, 1988], 112).

Jesus is our teacher when we wear His yoke. What does He want us to learn from Him on this subject? He desires us to know how to be meek and lowly in heart.

Christ showed us what it means to be meek by

never being weary in well-doing, by being patient in times of tribulation, and by submitting His will to the will of the Father in all things. Jesus knows what it is like to carry a yoke, one that is not easy, one that carries a burden that is anything but light. He carried His yoke without complaint and with total trust in His Father. Consider how He carried His cross, much like a yoke, on His remarkable shoulders so that our burden would be light. It is also noteworthy that He allowed another to assist Him in carrying that burden. Accepting assistance from others is one kind of meekness we can learn to ease the stress of carrying burdens.

The scriptures not only tell us of Christ's supreme meekness in all circumstances but also give us examples of those who learned to be meek and humble from His tutelage. Moses was described as "very meek, above all the men which were upon the face of the earth" (Numbers 12:3). This description of Moses was given *after* he delivered the children of Israel out of bondage, led them through the Red Sea, and camped with them in the wilderness.

"Meek," however, is not always the manner in which Moses was described. In reviewing the history of Israel with Jewish leaders in Jerusalem, Stephen spoke of Moses *before* he fled Egypt by explaining, "Pharaoh's daughter took him up, and nourished him for her own son. And Moses was learned in all the wisdom of the Egyptians, and *was mighty in words and in deeds*" (Acts 7:21–22; emphasis added). That is not typically the way we remember Moses. Mighty in words? Remember that God gave Moses a spokesman to assist him when Moses protested, "I am not eloquent, . . . but I am slow of speech, and of a slow tongue" (Exodus 4:10).

What happened to change Moses from being mighty in words to being slow of speech? I don't think Moses' ability to speak changed as much as his standard of greatness changed. Moses was taught by the Lord Himself, not at all like being taught by Pharaoh, even if it was in all the wisdom of the Egyptians. After receiving instruction from Jehovah, Moses exclaimed, "Now, . . . I know that man is nothing, which thing I never had supposed" (Moses 1:10). If we turn to worldly powers to receive instruction on how to carry burdens, we will become either arrogant and proud or self-deprecating and depressed. If we learn discipleship from Christ, we will become even as He is—meek and humble.

Meekness is rarely a characteristic we list among those we hope to obtain, and it is even less likely to be recognized by the world as evidence of success. President Howard W. Hunter wisely observed: "In a world too preoccupied with winning through intimidation and seeking to be number one, no large crowd is standing in line to buy books that call for mere meekness. But the meek shall inherit the earth, a pretty impressive corporate takeover—and done *without* intimidation! Sooner or later, . . . everyone will acknowledge that Christ's way is not only the *right* way, but ultimately the *only* way to hope and joy. Every knee shall bow and every tongue shall confess that gentleness is better than brutality, that kindness is greater than coercion, that the soft voice turneth away wrath" (*That We Might Have Joy* [Salt Lake City: Deseret Book, 1994], 9).

King Benjamin described meekness with several words that are closely related. Consider the cost of true discipleship in this list: "submissive, meek, humble, patient, full of love, willing to submit to all things which the Lord seeth fit to inflict upon him, even as a child doth submit to his father" (Mosiah 3:19). Did you also recognize another way the Lord teaches us these traits from this scripture? He taught us that becoming as little children increases our capacity to learn from Him. Most children are trusting, curious, eager to learn, instantly willing to volunteer to help—all characteristics that make the yoke of Christ easier.

Compare scenes from a typical day at church. Imagine yourself leading Sharing Time in Primary. You tell the children that you need a volunteer to say the prayer. What happens? You ask for someone to help you during singing time. What happens? Arms fly up and wave enthusiastically. Multiple voices plead, "Choose me! Choose me!" Now consider the same questions in a Gospel Doctrine class. As the teacher, you ask for a volunteer to say the prayer. You ask for help in reading a scripture. What happens? Heads go down. Eyes turn away. Silence is all too often the response you receive.

Several years ago at Brigham Young University, an unforgettable young man attended one of the classes I taught. The first day of class, I asked for a volunteer to offer a prayer. His hand immediately shot up. The second day, I made the same request. Again, this young man instantly raised his hand. The same thing occurred the third and fourth days. Finally, I asked him, "Why? What motivates you to volunteer every day? In all my years of teaching, I have never had a student so quick to volunteer." His reply was simple. As a deacon, he was taught by a quorum advisor to take every chance to volunteer service. The advisor then promised the young men that learning to volunteer would be a tremendous blessing in their lives. The now grown-up deacon had obviously never forgotten. That day, I saw in this student a type of Christ, who in turn taught me about the Savior. In premortality, the Father asked, "Whom shall I send?" There was one who did not hesitate. He reverently volunteered,

"Here am I, send me" (Abraham 3:27). Christ is meek; therefore, He submits His all to the Father. When I lack meekness, I do not trust the Lord in what He requires of me. I think that I can do it better. Consequently, I add unnecessary burdens to my load.

The Savior is the greatest example of meekness in yoke carrying. When we learn meekness from Him, we submit our all to God and gladly serve wherever and whenever He calls. As a result, His yoke becomes easy and His burden light.

Let us review five ways in which the Lord blesses us when we accept His yoke:

1. Taking Christ's yoke upon us prompts us to eliminate our sins and all other unnecessary burdens.

2. The Lord supports and sustains us in our responsibilities through covenants.

3. When we keep our covenants, we lift one another's burdens so they become light.

4. The Lord increases our strength and our
   ability to carry our load.
5. We learn to be meek and lowly in heart
   from Jesus Christ Himself.

"And I Will
Give You Rest"

The final concept in our passage in Matthew is the promise "and I will give you rest." After attempting to understand more fully the cost of discipleship, here portrayed as putting on the yoke of Jesus Christ, we almost forget about the promise. There are so many powerful blessings in the cost or requirements that the Lord asks of us that we realize that God has already showered us with promises. But God will still bestow the covenanted promise upon us when we faithfully cling to His yoke and diligently carry our responsibilities.

In addition to the miracles that occur in our life

by willingly taking on the yoke of Christ, God promises us "rest." Alma directed his son Helaman to teach his people "to never be weary of good works, but to be meek and lowly of heart; for such shall find rest to their souls" (Alma 37:34). The promise of rest is not restricted to the next life; the Lord promised us "peace in this world, and eternal life in the world to come" (D&C 59:23).

President Joseph F. Smith defined the Lord's rest as the peace that comes from unwavering faith in Christ and His doctrines. He wrote, "To my mind, [rest] means entering into the knowledge and love of God, having faith in his purpose and in his plan, to such an extent that we know we are right, and that we are not hunting for something else, we are not disturbed by every wind of doctrine, or by the cunning and craftiness of men who lie in wait to deceive. . . . The man [or woman] who has reached that degree of faith in God that all doubt and fear have been cast from him, he has entered into 'God's rest'" (*Gospel Doctrine* [Salt Lake City: Deseret Book, 1939], 58).

The blessed promise of rest restores our much-needed strength and energy to continue to carry our burdens with the sustaining power of the yoke of Christ. In other words, with the yoke of Christ and His blessing of rest, we are empowered to endure to the end.

Our Burdens
Will Be Light

As we come to better understand and appreciate Christ's enabling yoke, we begin to love the cost of discipleship as well as the promise. Christ has designed a kindly yoke for each us, made to fit our individual abilities and circumstances. It does not chafe and gouge but fortifies and protects. When we cheerfully receive His yoke as a gift and submit to the balanced load He commissions us individually to carry, there comes into our lives a renewed reverence and awe for our Redeemer and Deliverer. In a most powerful manner, we learn that He indeed loves us and empowers us in every possible way to become like Him.

Will we remember His yoke the next time we renew our covenant to strive to keep His commandments, take His name upon us, and always remember Him? It is reliance on His yoke that carries the guarantee that "[we] cannot fall" (Helaman 5:12) as we strive to stay upright in an increasingly disoriented world. Strengthened by faith in Christ, renewed in hope, and filled with the promise of His Spirit to always be with us, we will know rest through the assurance that we will successfully finish the course. And we will also be grateful for the journey.